Published By JC Publishers
714 North Sandsuky Ave
Upper Sandusky, Ohio 43351

The Shrewd Christian Business Woman
10 Steps For Success

© 2018 Betty Lok

No part of this book may be used or reproduced in any manner without written permission from publisher, except in context of reviews.

Every reasonable attempt has been made to identify owners of copyright. Errors or omissions will be corrected in subsequent editions.

Scripture taken from the HOLY BIBLE, NEW INTERNATIONAL VERSION® Copyright© 1973, 1978, 1984 by International Bible Society. Used by permission of Zondervan. All Rights Reserved.

Scripture quotations also taken from the New American Standard Bible® (NASB), Copyright © 1960, 1962, 1963, 1968, 1971, 1972, 1973, 1975, 1977, 1995 by The Lockman Foundation. Used by permission www.Lockman.org

ABOUT AUTHOR
Betty Lok is a chiropractor in Upper Sandusky, Ohio with twenty-five years' experience running a small business. Betty and Kevin Lok have two children, John David and Catherine Elizabeth.

BOOK DESIGNER
Brandon Mooney, Mooney Design

EDITORS
Avery Jennings
Michele Burch-Morehart
Catherine Lok
Desiree Young

TRANSCRIPTION
Wendy Brown

ARTIST
Trish Hill-Bellington

JC PUBLISHERS©

HOW TO BE A CHRISTIAN BUSINESS WOMAN

TABLE OF CONTENTS

Introduction	1

The Christian Business Woman | Part One

STEP ONE	GAIN	9
STEP TWO	NO GREED, NO CON	21
STEP THREE	PEOPLE BEFORE PRODUCTS	29
STEP FOUR	PLANNING	35
STEP FIVE	EMPLOYEES	41

The Christian Business Woman | Part Two

STEP SIX	HUSBANDS, BROTHERS, AND SISTERS	49
STEP SEVEN	DO THE RIGHT THING	55
STEP EIGHT	ACT	61
STEP NINE	BEING A BUSINESS<u>WOMAN</u>	71
STEP TEN	THANKFULNESS	79

Parting Blessing	83
Sample Business Plan	84
Appendix	90
Bibliography	100

The Shrewd Christian Business Woman

By Betty Jean Lok

HOW TO BE A CHRISTIAN BUSINESS WOMAN

Shrewd: **Having or showing sharp powers of judgment. Astute, sharp-witted, smart, acute, intelligent, clever, canny, perceptive, wise.**

"Look, I am sending you out as sheep among wolves. So be as shrewd as snakes and harmless as doves" (Matthew 10:16).

Have you ever wanted to possess the qualities of a snake? To be successful in business, we are to embrace the snake's shrewd powers to sense the business climate and to react. Yet, as Christian businesswomen, we are also called by Jesus to be like the gentle dove and not harm others in the process.

God commands us to be shrewd in business. Culture defines shrewdness as using deception for gain, so it seems incongruent that Jesus tells us to be shrewd. However, the real meaning of the word shrewd is showing sharp powers of judgment, being sharp-witted, intelligent, clever, and wise.

We are to be smart and make good decisions based on God-given perception, and our businesses will prosper. Being shrewd, as a Christian businesswoman, is an asset, and Jesus tells us to use this model. Christian businesswomen are called to use the cleverness of a snake and the innocence of the dove.

HOW TO BE A CHRISTIAN BUSINESS WOMAN

INTRODUCTION

Are you a businesswoman or are you thinking of starting a business? Being both a Christian and a businesswoman is possible *(Ecclesiastes 5:19)*. He has everything you need. God created the heavens and the earth, and He has the power to help guide you on your business adventure.

> **Ecclesiastes 5:19** – "And it is a good thing to receive wealth from God and the good health to enjoy it. To enjoy your work and accept your lot in life – this is indeed a gift from God."

To open, grow, and sustain your own business is exciting, fun, difficult, and freeing. God will never leave you or forsake you, but not everyone on this journey is on your side. Not everyone you encounter in your business wants your success. God comes with abundance, but the thief comes to damage and to attack your business. *"The thief comes only to steal and kill and destroy. I came that they may have life and have it to the full" **(John 10:10)***. Your business will exist in a world of deceit. Development of your

HOW TO BE A CHRISTIAN BUSINESS WOMAN

product will occur in the midst of "wolves." These wolves may come in the form of competition, your suppliers, and even some of your customers. These "wolves" can be hostile, for the purpose of their success and thus, your

Ladies, not everyone is your friend.

defeat. However, to be Christian businesswomen, we are called to be good, gentle, and harmless for success. *"God gave you your dream. Through Him all things were made; without Him, nothing was made that has been made"* ***(John 1:3).***

CHRISTIAN BUSINESSWOMEN

When did you first have your dream of being your own boss? Has God put the deep desire in your heart to run a business? Ladies, this means the dream in your heart, that deep spot of grace, was given to you as a gift from Jesus. He will light the love of your service.

Christ is in the title of this instruction manual. Model your life and business practices after His instructions, and God will promise success. *"I am the vine and you are the branches. If you remain in me and I in you, you will bear much fruit. Apart from me, you can do nothing"* ***(John 15:5).***

Ladies, your business has to be in the black, meaning you make a profit, or you will not have a business for long. Your business model and your life have to remain in the light to have a rich and satisfying life this side of Heaven.

Of course, you may stumble and lose money along the way. These lessons are painful. Your feelings may get hurt. You also may feel

Psalm 37:24 – "Though he may stumble, he will not fall, for the Lord upholds him with His hand."

INTRODUCTION

taken advantage of; hang in there! My wish for you is that the wisdom contained in these pages may keep you from falling *(Psalm 37:24).*

WHAT IS YOUR BUSINESS?

Spiritwood, North Dakota, where I grew up, is a town of about 20 houses with one bar and an old brick schoolhouse.

The schoolhouse included 28 students, three teachers, one of which doubled as the principal, a janitor who put coal in the furnace, and a cook who made soft, chewy chocolate chip cookies from scratch. As the largest class in the school, we had five students. We had three recesses a day and grew up outside, playing softball by ourselves, raking leaves into outlines of our dream houses, building snow forts, and sledding.

While walking the prairies, I was fascinated by the animal bones God let me find. My love grew into exploration and fascination in a field where I study every bump, crevice, and curve of each vertebra.

As a teenager, I suffered with migraines. After x-rays, CAT scans, and angiograms of the brain which were scary and painful, traditional medicine had no answers. Then, my mom took me to a chiropractor. He explained that my neck vertebrae were out of alignment from a fall down the stairs at Grandma's house, making my nerves angry.

Now, I am a chiropractor who owns my own small business in Ohio in the United States of America. I absolutely love it! I also want you to love what you do. If God put a love in your heart, it is there for a reason, and Jesus expects you to fulfill your purpose to completion. I enjoy spending time working on the spine and helping people. What do you want to spend your time doing? What is your awe-inspiring, unique love that is not work, but enjoyable for you? That is your business!

This is a book of business and how to be successful as a Christian businesswoman. In Part I, you will learn the business of being a

HOW TO BE A CHRISTIAN BUSINESS WOMAN

Christian businesswoman. In Part II, you will learn how to be a Christian woman running her business. *Are you ready?*

PRE-EMPTIVE STRIKE

Many business owners like to be their own bosses, but Christian businesswomen are unique; we work for God. God wants you to do business for Him. God will give you the use of your time and talents for His purpose and for good works.

Before beginning your business, you must be willing to place God's

> **Proverbs 1:7** – "The fear of the Lord is the beginning of knowledge, but fools despise wisdom and instruction."

will above your own. Your preemptive strike for success is to fear God. God paid a large price for your opportunity in business, through His son Jesus' blood. God's love for us is shown by redeeming sin, including that of Christian businesswomen by payment through His Son's death.

When we do not use the gifts He has given us and has created for us, it lets God down and does not praise Him. *"For there is one God and one Mediator between God and mankind, the man Jesus Christ, who gave Himself as a ransom for all people. This now has been witnessed to at the proper time" (1Timothy 2:5-6).*

So how do we honor and fear our almighty God? Do what He has been telling you to do!

If you have a business idea, whether it is new or an idea that you've had for a long time, it is never too late. The most effectual

What is ransom?

A sum of payment demanded for the release of a prisoner.

INTRODUCTION

means to your business success is calling upon the name of the Almighty. Call on God's divine assistance. If you are within His will, the power in you can be God's power. Align your business model to follow God's plan. God will honor your effort.

What does the **fear of God mean**? It means to acknowledge, honor, and respect God, to be in awe of His power, and to obey His word.

SHREWDNESS

"Look, I am sending you out as sheep among wolves. So be as shrewd as snakes and harmless as doves" **(Matthew 10:16)**. Ladies, we are called to be sharp, intelligent, clever, and wise; not gullible pawns or deceitful in business.

We are commanded to be shrewd!

The Parable of the Shrewd Manager

Jesus told His disciples: "There was a rich man whose manager was accused of wasting his possessions. So he called him in and asked him, 'What is this I hear about you? Give an account of your management, because you cannot be manager any longer.'

"The manager said to himself, 'What shall I do now? My master is taking away my job. I'm not strong enough to dig, and I'm ashamed to beg – I know what I'll do so that, when I lose my job here, people will welcome me into their houses.'

"So he called in each one of his master's debtors. He asked the first, 'How much do you owe my master?'

"'Nine hundred gallons of olive oil,' he replied.

"The manager told him, 'Take your bill, sit down quickly, and make it

HOW TO BE A CHRISTIAN BUSINESS WOMAN

four hundred and fifty.'

"Then he asked the second, 'And how much do you owe?'

"'A thousand bushels of wheat,' he replied.

"He told him, 'Take your bill and make it eight hundred.'

"The master commended the dishonest manager because he had acted shrewdly. For the people of this world are more shrewd in dealing with their own kind than are the people of the light. I tell you, use worldly wealth to gain friends for yourselves, so that when it is gone, you will be welcomed into eternal dwellings.

Whoever can be trusted with very little can also be trusted with much, and whoever is dishonest with very little will also be dishonest with much. So if you have not been trustworthy in handling worldly wealth, who will trust you with true riches? And if you have not been trustworthy with someone else's property, who will give you property of your own?

No one can serve two masters. Either you will hate the one and love the other, or you will be devoted to the one and despise the other. You cannot serve both God and money" (**Luke 16:1-14)**.

In this world, we are given God's resources to use, and if we cannot be trusted with resources such as: money, wealth, property, and goods, that in the eternal realm means nothing, so how can God trust us with our own property in eternity?

Christian women are to be smart, perceptive, and clever in using the world's currency for good – to help people. Furthermore, Jesus states that we cannot serve two masters. Remember, the preemptive strike in your business is to honor God above all.

Our business practices must line up with God's to have eternal benefit. How we run our business now will have eternal consequences.

If we are Christian businesswomen and do a good job following God's

INTRODUCTION

precepts, He promises that when we are faithful with a little, He is going to allow us to be faithful in heaven with much.

Let us go to Step 1. §

HOW TO BE A CHRISTIAN BUSINESS WOMAN

PART ONE

STEP ONE | GAIN

There is something right and true when your business does well: jobs are created, and your product helps people. The common denominator of all business is money. Money is not evil. It is a tool. The world defines gain as currency – money – but God's idea of gain may be different for you. The currency God may want you to gain may include not merely financial blessing, but also a lesson in humility, wisdom, and kindness.

Early in my career, I was overly confident. Within a year, our little business was successful, and the town had elected me to a public office.

I thought to myself, "Everything I touch turns to gold." Scarily convicted, I knew immediately that I was soon in for a humbling "detention." Within a few years, I was taught obedience through being named as part of the school board in a lawsuit, attended two student funerals as a member of the school board, and closed our first office location.

The world teaches us that power, prestige, and fame are favored,

HOW TO BE A CHRISTIAN BUSINESS WOMAN

but God has allowed me to see the single mom working three jobs and still getting her children ready for school possesses honorable perseverance. The hurting husband and father that has just finished six "twelve- hour days" and has done so for the last twenty years is a real hero.

The business climate puts a premium on greed, getting rich quick, and cutting corners to save a buck. In many ways, it is touted as good to lie if it increases the bottom line. A law student once told me the final settlement is what matters, not how you get there. In his view, the end justifies the means. That is not God's way.

In the Bible, God's first commandment to His people is *"You shall have no other gods before me"* ***(Deuteronomy 5:7 & Exodus 20:3)***.

This includes money. "All profit belongs to God; we merely borrow and manage God's limitless resources" ***(Psalm 24:1)***.

> **Psalm 24:1** – "The earth is the Lord's and everything in it, the world, and all who live in it."

BUSINESS IS GOOD

Creating a business is good. Business brings health and prosperity to a community by the influx of the world's currency.

Businesses provide employment for full-time, part-time, and contract employees. Jobs provide income for employees to buy the necessities for their families. When businesses suffer, communities diminish through increased crime, property devaluation, and declining schools.

As Christian businesswomen, we not only bring money and prosperity to our families and communities, but we also offer God's currency – love. We show God's love through our hard work and daily sacrifices for our customers and businesses. The Christian businesswoman who prays over the customer that she is serving with her gift of pedicures, or the massage therapist at the end of the session that says, "Don't give

PART ONE | STEP ONE – GAIN

up," after listening to her client's troubled life both exhibit their Godly love through service.

> **1 John 1-11** – "Dear Friends, since God so loved us, we also ought to love each other."

As a Christian businesswoman, you will develop and grow in leadership and influence over others, and how you carry yourself in kindness, strength, and righteousness exhibits God's wisdom. Use your new-found and hard-won gifts to lead your community and society in other areas such as service organizations, city councils, and corporate boards. God's love is expressed by loving our customers and expressing that love through our business.

Good gain is advantageous. God is multiplying, and He expects you to do the best you can with His resources. But not all gain is good…

NOT ALL GAIN IS GOOD

> **Proverbs 1:19** – "Such are the paths of all who go after ill-gotten gain; it takes away the life of those who get it."

There are two types of gain: good gain and ill-gotten gain. Ill-gotten gain is deadly, and it will destroy you ***(Proverbs 1:19)***. In our businesses, we cannot expect to build with deception and take away God's shining gift of abundance. As Christian businesswomen, we are not to utilize the tools of deception and greed and expect God's financial blessings and business success.

Dishonest methods used to obtain business goals is not being

Ill-gotten gain: Splendid qualities prostituted to low purpose.

HOW TO BE A CHRISTIAN BUSINESS WOMAN

shrewd; it is disobedient and disregards our God. The methods used to accomplish our business goals are as important as the result.

For example, a company once came to me and promised that if I would rent a room to them, they would provide nerve tests to my patients. An adjustment cost in the office is an average of $32. The nerve testing charges from this company would have been over $2,000 for each patient. While the rental income of an extra $200 a month would have been nice to a new cash-strapped business, to subject patients to unneeded, expensive tests would have resulted in an ill-reputation.

When we make our profit with deceit, greed, and poor quality, our profit will not last. **Proverbs 10:2** states that, *"Ill-gotten treasures have no lasting value."*

We cannot make devilish deals and expect our businesses to flourish. When starting and growing a business, if one does not pay his suppliers or shortchanges his customers, the business may prosper short-term, but it will not last.

Jeremiah 22:13 also warns, *"Woe to him who builds his house without righteousness and his upper rooms without justice, who uses his neighbors' services without pay and does not give him his wages."*

We cannot gain our success by dishonesty in our business. We, as Christian businesswomen, are different. We are to build our businesses with integrity. Our business can provide for our home and family. However, if we choose to use the world's standard of deceptiveness and dishonesty, the Bible tells us that sorrow will await. One cannot expect blessings from disobedience. And ***Habakkuk 2:9*** reminds us, *"What sorrow awaits you who build big houses with money gained dishonestly! You believe your wealth will buy you security, putting your family's nest beyond the reach of danger."*

> **1 Timothy 6:9** – "Those who want to get rich fall into temptation and a trap and into many foolish and harmful desires that plunge people into ruin and destruction."

PART ONE | STEP ONE – GAIN

Once our business is up and running, if we take the bait of cheaper parts and inferior products for a greater profit, our customers will soon determine that they have been deceived. The products are no longer worth the cost. Our once stellar reputation is now blemished as expensive and a "scam." If you want to get rich quick, this is not the book for you *(1 Timothy 6:9)*.

Lasting wealth is made honestly, little by little. *"Dishonest money dwindles away, but whoever gathers money little by little makes it grow" (Proverbs 13:11)*.

> **Matthew 19:23** – "Then Jesus said to His disciples, 'Truly I tell you it is hard for someone who is rich to enter the kingdom of heaven.'"

Jesus warns us about the desire to be rich. Ladies, if you want to rain ruin and destruction onto your lives, or if you want to have a hard time getting into heaven, focus on the desire to be rich.

If you want to succeed in your business, focus on what you are doing and why you are doing it. When you get off track and your business diminishes, go back to your first love.

For me, that is focusing on doing the best adjustment I can for the product of "healing and health without drugs or surgery." For instance, my business is chiropractic natural healthcare, healing by aligning bones to increase blood and nerve flow to the body. If my clinic's focus diverts to "laser hair removal or the sale of beauty products," the lure of further riches will ultimately take my energy away from the prosperous portion of the business.

HOW TO BE A CHRISTIAN BUSINESS WOMAN

Your job through your business is to spill life lavishly, sacrificially for the glory of God and the good of man. If your focus and desire is to serve others, you will have success.

EXPECTATIONS OF JESUS — I AM AN EXACTING MAN

One day, Jesus was walking in Jericho on his way to Jerusalem the week before His last seven days on earth. Zacchaeus, meaning honest and pure, was a man who did not live up to his name. He was a rich, crooked traitor who was the chief Jewish tax collector for Rome. Tax collectors made themselves rich by gouging their fellow Jews. The greedy businessman Zacchaeus was short and wanted to see Jesus, so he climbed a sycamore-fig tree because he could not see over the crowd.

Did You Know?
Jerusalem is 15.9 miles from Jericho.

Jesus said, *"Zacchaeus, come down immediately. I must stay at your house today"* **(Luke 19:5)**.

Paraphrasing, the subjects in Jerusalem said, "Whoa! This is not fair! Zacchaeus is robbing us blind!"

Zacchaeus replied, "Wait! I am going to give half of my money to the poor, and if I have cheated anyone, I am going to pay them back quadruple!"

Jesus said, "I came to look for you and came to save you, because you were lost, but now you understand."

What Is A Sycamore-fig Tree?
It is an ancient, fruit-producing tree, and the leaves resemble those of a mulberry tree.

Then, on the way to Zacchaeus' house, Jesus started explaining what His servants should do with the money.

PART ONE | STEP ONE – GAIN

How Should Christian Women Use Money?

He said: "A man of noble birth went to a distant country to have himself appointed king and then to

What Is A Mina?
A mina means three months' pay.

return. So he called ten of his servants and gave them ten minas. 'Put this money to work,' he said, 'until I come back.'

"But his subjects hated him and sent a delegation after him to say, 'We don't want this man to be our king.'

"He was made king, however, and returned home. Then he sent for the servants to whom he had given the money in order to find out what they had gained with it.

"The first one came and said, 'Sir, your mina has earned ten more.'

"'Well done, my good servant!' his master replied. 'Because you have been trustworthy in a very small matter, take charge of ten cities.'

"The second came and said, 'Sir, your mina has earned five more.'

"His master answered, 'You take charge of five cities.'

"Then another servant came and said, 'Sir, here is your mina; I have kept it laid away in a piece of cloth. I was afraid of you because you are a hard man. You take what you did not put in and reap what you did not sow.'

"His master replied, 'I will judge you by your own words, you wicked servant!' You knew, did you, that I am a hard man, taking out what I did

HOW TO BE A CHRISTIAN BUSINESS WOMAN

not put in and reaping what I did not sow? Why, then, didn't you put my money on deposit, so that when I came back I could have collected it with interest?'

"Then he said to those standing by, 'Take his mina away from him and give it to the one who has ten minas.'

"'Sir,' they said, 'he already has ten!'

"He replied, 'I tell you that to everyone who has, more will be given, but as for the one who has nothing, even what they have will be taken away. But those enemies of mine who did not want me to be king over them – bring them here and kill them in front of me'" **(Luke 19:12-27)**.

There are two groups of people in this story: the ruler's servants and the subjects who did not want the boss to be their king.

The ruler deals with his servants first. Remember, he gave the command to put this money to work! They were all given two-and-a-half years' pay! One did great; the first servant doubled the master's investment.

The second servant increased his master's money by 50 percent. But the third businessman was afraid to act.

The third servant did not share his master's interests. He did not do anything with his opportunity. Our Creator's intentions are good and our God is a genuine God. God wants to see His creation succeed and prosper. One way to contribute in today's social structure is to be successful in business. God will use your opportunity of leadership and management for the good of His world. You have an integral role as a Christian businesswoman when you do well and your business benefits mankind; this praises God.

But sometimes, we struggle and even fail. God sent His Son to help us. Your true value is based on God's estimate of your worth. You belong to Him. God created you and wants to see you succeed. He has given

PART ONE | STEP ONE – GAIN

you all the tools that you need. Try your best and work diligently. Like the third servant, the tools and resources were available and perfectly placed. If you fail, take an honest look and ask if you really worked your hardest before you go whining back to God. As a Christian businesswoman, there is a time to stop asking God for help and to act.

Servant Three was too scared to act. The mina parable, in part, is saying that fear cannot be used as an excuse not to do what God has determined as your service. My fellow beloved sisters, is God really your Boss if you do not fulfill your purpose? Do not use fear as an excuse not to start your business, continue working, or expand your corporation.

We, as Christian businesswomen, must use the financial gifts God gave us for the prospering of our businesses – His work.

Jesus then reveals that the subjects who did not want to be ruled by their king were killed.

We can learn from this group, too. As we gain financial prosperity, we cannot not to lose sight of God, our CEO.

Business Commands	Business Blessings	Warnings
Genesis 9:7	**2 Corinthians 9:10**	**Proverbs 28:20**
Increase	He will give you what you need. He will increase your profits (harvest).	You will get punished if you want to get rich quick.
		Luke 12:15 Watch out for greed.

HOW TO BE A CHRISTIAN BUSINESS WOMAN

> **Philippians 4:6** – "Do not be anxious about anything, but in every situation, by prayer and petition, present your request to God."

WHAT IF I FAIL?

The biggest fear in starting your small business is financial ruin. But, successful businesswomen are not paralyzed by worry. Indeed, Jesus commands us not to worry *(Philippians 4:6)*.

The successful Christian businesswomen with whom I have had conversations with have felt that when they started their businesses, they were simply obeying God by doing what they were supposed to do. They planned, chose love and obedience, worked hard, and had faith. You have two choices: love or fear. So plan, but do not worry.

Remember, gain is good in business, and if your business fails, there is also knowledge to be gained by failure.

Once, a salesman came into the office selling a special blue fluorescent light bulb for the patient rooms. He promised that the patients would recover quicker

"I just wish all my mistakes weren't so expensive!"

and that the business would grow. With excitement, I replaced all the white tubes with the blue tubes, which were three times as expensive. however, the patients did not flock in and the lights did not seem to relax the patients or improve the treatment outcome.

When you fail, you will develop quickness and prudence in dealings with things temporal. My wish is that you do not have to undergo failure and defeat, but that He blesses you with prosperity. God also wants to tell you that it will be well with you! *"Tell the righteous it will be well with them, for they will enjoy the fruits of their deeds"* ***(Isaiah 3:10)***.

PART ONE | STEP ONE – GAIN

So, let us say that the worst-case scenario is business failure. What should you do? First of all, learn from your mistakes so that you do not make the same ones. Trust God; He will straighten your path. Be grateful for what you do have.

When you get snookered – and you will – the great news is that God is there. He delights in all of our ways. *"For the Lord takes delight in His people: He crowns the humble with victory"* **(Psalm 149:4)**.

Applicable Verses	Actions To Do When You Fail
Jeremiah 8:4	Get up!
Proverbs 24:16	Get up!
Proverbs 26:11	Do not keep making the same mistakes.
Psalm 119:71	Learn to obey.
Psalm 40:23	Be grateful for what you have.
Proverbs 3:5-6	Trust God fully.
2 Timothy 1-7	Love.

So what step can be used to better your chances of business success? Step 2! §

HOW TO BE A CHRISTIAN BUSINESS WOMAN

STEP TWO

WHERE THERE IS NO GREED, THERE IS NO CON

There was once a lady who lived in Eden. God planted a luscious garden in eastern Eden. With access, she could eat as much as she wanted, whenever she wanted.

A river flowed out of Eden to water the garden. The garden was bursting with gorgeous trees that dripped with fruit that was a feast to her eyes. In the center of the garden, there were two trees. One was the tree of life and the other was the tree of knowledge of both good and evil.

"And the Lord God commanded the man, 'You are free to eat from any tree in the garden; but you must not eat from the tree of the knowledge of good and evil, for when you eat from it, you will surely die' " ***(Genesis 2:16-17).***

In the beginning, Eve became greedy. Her eye desired the one delicious fruit that oozed promise of god-like wisdom. Paraphrasing, her Creator, Provider, and Protector loved her enough to tell her, "Do not touch it. Just having the knowledge of evil is enough to kill you."

HOW TO BE A CHRISTIAN BUSINESS WOMAN

"Now, the serpent was more crafty than any of the wild animals the Lord God had made. He said to the woman, 'Did God really say, "You must not eat from any tree in the garden?"' The woman responded to the serpent, 'We may eat fruit from the tree in the garden, but God did say, "You must not eat fruit from the tree that is in the middle of the garden, and you must not touch it, or you will die."'

"'You will certainly not die,' the serpent said to the woman. 'For God knows that when you eat from it, your eyes will be opened, and you will be like God, knowing good and evil'" **(Genesis 3:1-5)**.

The serpent convinced her that God did not have her best interest at heart.

"When the woman saw that the fruit of the tree was good for food and pleasing to the eye, and also desirable for gaining wisdom, she took some of it and ate and she also gave some to her husband who was with her, and he ate it" **(Genesis 3:6)**.

That sneaky, lying serpent! Eve wanted to be like God, knowing good and evil. In your business, look to all the "trees and fruit" of which you have been given. Greed will give the serpent an opening. Actively and intentionally going against the right, good, and true actions because of an appetite for food, money, prosperity, power, and the world's wisdom are put in your path by the serpent to hurt your business, and the pain can extend to those you love.

Where there is no greed, there is no con.

BE WISE; DO NOT BE FOOLISH

When we get snookered in business, we cannot blame the serpent because we were unobservant. God wants us to think wisely. Do not rely on emotional responses for your business decisions. Eve's emotional response was, "I will like the yummy fruit from the tree of knowledge of good and evil."

PART ONE | STEP TWO – NO GREED/NO CON

Today, Christian businesswomen can choose the blessings and fulfillment that comes with obeying God. God wants us to be wise, not to be tricked by serpents, business partners, lawyers, customers, bankers, and competitors. Do not let your failures limit your future success.

Similarly, being overly nice in business does not mean your suppliers and business associates will treat you in kind or "give you a better deal." Channel the astuteness of the snake with time-sensitive business dealings and contracts. God will give you perception for your business.

While waiting to board a flight at the airport, I once overhead a businessman on the phone talking to one of his managers about a customer and one of the businessman's employees.

The businessman was talking about a "real nice customer" that was "easy-going." On the other end of the phone, the manager expressed concerns to the business owner about the service personnel assigned to the "really nice customer." The manager went on to explain that the service personnel assigned to this customer was slow in the performance of his duties.

The business owner almost bragged that he did not mind or care as the customer was "so nice" that they would make more money off him by charging greater billable hours by sending in an incompetent worker.

The wolves in the business world will look upon you and your business as an easy target and someone to "take a bite out of." Do not be a tasty little morsel. God commands us to be knowledgeable. Be kind, but do not be naive in your business dealings. God expects us to face reality and does not leave us without the tools of the clever snake while maintaining consideration and amiability.

As Christian business owners, we should not throw pearls before swine. *"Do not give dogs what is sacred; do not throw your pearls to pigs. If you do, they may trample them under their feet, and then turn and tear you to pieces"* **(Matthew 7:6)**.

HOW TO BE A CHRISTIAN BUSINESS WOMAN

In business, this means: do not sell your product or service for less than it is worth. Customers will not value your products or services if you give them away. Charge a fair price, or you will not be in business for long.

PIE!

You will be tempted to take others' pie. Other businessmen and businesswomen will also want to take some of your pie.

The secret: there is enough pie for everyone. Ladies, if you want too much "pie," you will not sleep well *(Ecclesiastes 5:12)*.

> **Ecclesiastes 5:12** – "The sleep of a laborer is sweet, whether he eats little or much, but as for the rich, their abundance permits them no sleep."

Customers like pie, too, so you will need to teach them to place a value on what it is you do. When your clients, customers, or patients want something for nothing, it is called greed – pure and simple – as they want you to give away valuable goods and services. For instance, if you have an open house and generously give away a sample of your product and your possible future customer says, "I want two," be shrewd to ascertain the motive behind the request. There are some customers that will not be healthy for you or your business and will be better served by others.

We are not supposed to treat the rich better than the poor or the poor better than the rich. *"Do not pervert justice; do not show partiality to the poor or favoritism to the great, but judge your neighbor fairly"* ***(Leviticus 19:15)***.

PART ONE | STEP TWO – NO GREED/NO CON

However, we are supposed to take care of the poor, and to do this, you may want to have a sliding fee scale. If you are in a service business, this is common.

> **Luke 6:38** – "Give, and it will be given to you. A good measure, pressed down, shaken together, and running over, will be poured into your lap. For the measure you use, it will be measured to you."

In regards to your business and giving back from the abundance God grants, the New Testament has very clear instructions. We are to be generous, and it will be given back to us overflowing *(Luke 6:38)*.

THE TRAP OF FREE MONEY

Asking God for free money is not right, instead ask God for the development of your gifts and talents. Then, the coins will follow.

Halfway through chiropractic college, I found myself without enough money to buy milk and food for my nine-month-old son. I was offered food stamps, free baby milk through a government program, money for our apartment, and yet more just to live on. The only catch: they required me to stay poor in order to keep receiving these gifts.

With gratitude, I accepted the free grocery card for my son's infant formula. The apartment stipend, gas money, and food stamps I declined. It would have been nice not to take out as many school loans, to have had meat and vegetables instead of onions and eggs for months straight; but with a warning in my heart, I could not.

It would have been easy to accept the "manna" of government assistance, but it would have been a trap with one hand reaching through the bars. To continue with free money, I would have had to ignore my dream of being a chiropractor and give up my calling to own a business; I could have lost my purpose.

HOW TO BE A CHRISTIAN BUSINESS WOMAN

"Free" money is not free. It is taken from other workers. If you are capable of working, accepting free money is a form of greed. It is good to get up and go to work. It is a trap to the human spirit not to work if God made us able. In return for the "free" money, you give away your soul, spirit, and future. The "free" money is not enough to live on, but just enough to develop an addiction.

A government may impose an addiction to free money without the common interest of a cure. Free money takes the hope out of life by stagnating achievement and depleting self-worth and pride.

"Whatever your hands find to do, do it with all your might, for in the realm of the dead, where you are going, there is neither working nor planning nor knowledge nor wisdom" **(Ecclesiastes 9:10)**.

UNEQUAL WEIGHTS

Selling your customer less than you promise is also greed. *"Differing weights and differing measures, both of them are abominable to the Lord"* **(Proverbs 20:10)**. Many companies cheat customers in the name of cost effectiveness. Making a cheaper product and selling it to the customer based on the original quality is a horror to God; His word calls this a dishonest scale. Business culture can lead employers to make the mistake of looking at short-term profits over long-term company health, gain, and stability.

In the USA, the government is in charge of weights and measures. When we are filling up our gas tanks, we can assume that we are getting a full gallon of gas, because of a government official's signature on the pump. *"The Lord detests dishonest scales, but with accurate weights find favor with Him"* **(Proverbs 11:1)**.

An **abomination** means something obscene, evil, criminal, and loathsome.

PART ONE | STEP TWO – NO GREED/NO CON

Using unequal weights is an abomination to the Lord. Christian businesswomen are called not only to reject greed and dishonesty, but also to give more than expected. A Christian business is not harmful; it is wholesome, nonirritating, inoffensive, and reliable.

Extol means to praise Christ enthusiastically through your work.

GOOD MEASURE

To be a Christian businesswoman, extol Christian principles in your business. Be generous, do more than is expected, be overflowing in your work, products, and dealings.

God is adamant about being honest in business. *"Lying lips are an abomination to the Lord, but those who deal faithfully are His delight"* ***(Proverbs 12:22)***. For example, if your customer has a credit, return it. It is their money!

Good business allows for the florist to generously add an extra piece of baby's breath to an arrangement or for the baker to make 13 treats in a dozen. Christian women can be instinctively generous in business measures.

My friend, a Christian factory supervisor, said it this way: "I want to encourage my coworkers and fellow employees to provide a good product at the end of the assembly line. I want the customer to get what they paid for." §

HOW TO BE A CHRISTIAN BUSINESS WOMAN

STEP THREE

PEOPLE BEFORE PRODUCTS

People are more valuable than your product. The products of this world are temporary. Plastic degrades; services are forgotten; the realtor's house is demolished.

Putting your customers, your employees, and even yourself before your product, profit, and business can be difficult. Jesus wants us to put people –our customers and employees– first. When we treat our fellow human beings with kindness, generosity, and forgiveness, we honor our Maker.

For example, a front desk receptionist refilled a coffee pot that was sitting next to the TV receiver and phone system. A fellow employee had already filled the water receptacle and the coffee overflowed, short circuiting the new TV system, a $300 error. The employee was not reprimanded financially, as it was an honest mistake. Unforeseen expenses are a part of the cost of doing business. Employees are more important than the equipment replacement cost.

HOW TO BE A CHRISTIAN BUSINESS WOMAN

Next to the Blessed Sacrament itself, your neighbor is the holiest object presented to your senses. If he is your Christian neighbor, he is holy in almost the same way, for in him also Christ *vere latititat*, which is Latin for "truly hides," – the glorifier and the glorified, Glory Himself, is truly hidden.[1]

Principles of a Christian Business Owner
People must come before products!
1. Do the right thing.
2. Do not take what is not yours.
3. Do not wish for what other people have.
4. Be honest.
5. Use just scales.[2]

THE PRODUCT MUST BE GOOD AND YOU MUST BELIEVE IN IT

My purpose is to be a chiropractor. God gave me the ability to adjust, and I am absolutely in awe of the innate healing power of the human body and spirit. The spine is both complicated and beautiful. It supports the weight of our bodies and allows us to walk the sacred earth and to bend at the feet of Jesus to serve.

---

[1] (C.S. Lewis, The Weight of Glory, in the The Weight of Glory and Other Addresses [New York: HarperOne, 2001]) 36,46

[2] The Life Application Study Bible New International Version Study Note
Notes and Bible Helps copyright ©1986 owned by assignment by Tyndale House Publishers, Inc.
Harmony of Gospels copyright ©1986 by James C. Galvin. All Rights reserved. Used by permission of Tyndale House Publishers, Inc

PART ONE | STEP THREE – PEOPLE BEFORE PRODUCTS

Did you know that Jesus was a chiropractor, too? ☺

"... And a woman was there who had been crippled by a spirit for 18 years. She was bent over and could not straighten up at all. When Jesus saw her, He called her forward and said to her, 'Woman, you are set free from your infirmity.' Then He put His hands on her, and immediately she straightened up and praised God" **(Luke 13:11)**.

Being involved in a business that provides worthwhile products or services is important. Many bright businesswomen take advantage of the business systems and practices of this world to enrich themselves. However, your business should be built on a standard of excellence and integrity.

> **Matthew 5:48** – "Be perfect, therefore, as your heavenly Father is perfect."

God wants us to produce the best and to excel. He wants our products and services to be of excellent quality. Remember that God has prepared work in advance for us to do. When we connect with what He has made us to do, we can go into His mission field with a sense of purpose.

What if you are selling something that a buyer does not want? Jesus has very clear instructions about what we should do with customers, suppliers, and/or employees that do not want what we have to offer.

Jesus sent out His disciples with a purpose, but some of the towns they visited did not want what they offered: to heal the sick, raise the dead, and to give freely. *"...Freely you have received; freely give." (Matthew 10:8)*

> **Matthew 10:14** – "If anyone will not welcome you or listen to your words, leave that home or town and shake the dust off your feet."

HOW TO BE A CHRISTIAN BUSINESS WOMAN

The lesson here is to not keep going back to the customers, suppliers, and companies that do not want to work with you and have no desire for what you have to offer.

When I first came to the small rural town where I now run my business, I assumed with pride that local businesses would want to sell me paint, carpet, and office supplies and would thank me for my business. However, they did not want my business and did not seem thrilled that a newcomer was in their town; I did not return.

As I came to town to become part of the community and to get my business name out, I wanted to join a local men's group of which I had been a part in another state. At the time, this national men's service organization had never had women as part of their group in this location. I respected and accepted their charter and guidelines and considered, "Why would I want to be a part of an organization that did not want me?" I found other ways to serve and instead ran for the school board instead.

Your products and services are valuable. If your customer does not want your product or services, or if a supplier does not want to work with you, shake the dust off your feet and move on. Search for those that do recognize your worth.

HONORING YOUR CUSTOMER

In my business, I am honored to serve. Healing is the product. Jesus was very clear about healing. He honored His creation by giving them a choice.

In medical terms, this is called patient autonomy. Doctors, dentists, physician assistants, and nurse practitioners practice this Biblical

PART ONE | STEP THREE – PEOPLE BEFORE PRODUCTS

concept daily. Christian professionals and businesswoman should respect the patient or customer before profit.

Patient autonomy is defined as the innate worth of a patient and their choice in regard to treatment and to their health. When a blind man was encountered, Jesus did not assume that the man wanted to receive his sight *(Luke 18:41)*.

Instead, Jesus asked the man who could not see and then had the love, compassion, and kindness to let the man choose.

Some Christian business organizations lose the Biblical teaching in regards to asking before doing. Well-intentioned Christians go into neighborhoods and countries and put our values and ideas upon that community.

For instance, generous members of my church had an idea to build a pigpen to provide meat for a village in Central America. They built the pigpen, provided a pig, and left.

However, they failed to consult their customer in that the water source was a two-mile walk from the village. The pig died one month after the committee left.

We did not ask; if we would have, we would have realized that the villagers were surrounded by wild pigs to eat and had no need for pigpens.

We as Christian businesswomen must ask, not assume. After further consideration, on a second mission trip, the servants of our church went back and built the village a well. The needs of the customer were placed first, and therefore, it was a prosperous service. §

> **Luke 18:41** – "What do you want Me to do for you?"
> "Lord, I want to see" he replied.

HOW TO BE A CHRISTIAN BUSINESS WOMAN

STEP FOUR

PLANNING

COUNTING THE COST

Luke 14:28 – "Suppose one of you wants to build a tower. Won't you first sit down and estimate the cost to see if you have enough money to complete it?"

Before making a business decision, sit down and count the cost *(Luke 14:28)*. God expects us to have faith and be all in spiritually and financially.

During your planning process, if you are unsure on how to proceed or if to proceed, do the following two things:

1. Ask God.

2. Ask others for help.

HOW TO BE A CHRISTIAN BUSINESS WOMAN

"Plans fail for lack of counsel, but with many advisers they succeed" **(Proverbs 15:22).**

God knows what you need, and He will put people in your path that will help you determine His best road for your business. Obey God's instructions and whatever He tells you to do, and your business will be better than you ever dreamed.

Once my husband and I got our first business up and running, we wanted to open a second location. Having used all of my husband's seed money for our first business, I had to come up with more money to open the second office. I went to Jerry, a banker, and we sat down together in his sunlit office and counted the cost.

There is no such thing as a stupid question!

"God, should I buy the extra-soft perfumed toilet paper or the durable toilet paper for my customers?"

I sat across from his desk and listened as he explained that I needed a business plan, collateral, and a small business loan. The business plan, he went on to explain, had to include profit/loss statements and long-term planning.

With hard work and much consideration, I prepared inventory, profit expectations, competition analysis, and a long-term vision to meet the expected growth model. Along with collateral of my husband's income as an electrical engineer, we were able to obtain the loan!

Twenty-three years later, Jerry stopped me one day at the same bank where it all started and asked me how everything had gone. I explained that God had been generous, as we started out with two little rooms in a small office space to our current two offices with thirteen employees. How thankful I was to the banker.

He then gave me a kiss on the cheek in the main lobby of the bank. It was a fatherly kindness bestowed upon an appreciative lady. I smiled, turned and walked out of the bank with a tear running down my cheek.

PART ONE | STEP FOUR – PLANNING

In one simple gesture, Jerry showed me love, gratitude, and gentle kindness, as if to say he was proud of how the business had grown after our initial meeting.

TIME IS MONEY

How much is your time worth?

Once you are making money, take an honest look at the value of your time. If you have a business report due and you are paid $100 per hour, but also have laundry and a home to clean, it makes sense to hire someone to help you. To fold laundry will cost about an hour of labor. By hiring help with the housecleaning you will be ahead by $80 and be more productive.

A clean home requires much energy and time. It is important to have a peaceful, organized, and restful home. If it takes six hours each week to clean your home, your business production will increase by hiring someone to assist you with your home responsibilities.

Not only are you blessed with more time, but a job is also provided.

There is something good and true about working with our hands, and one job is not more important than another in God's eyes. Housekeepers are businesswomen, too! Each of us serves with different gifts. Use your gifts!

> **Romans 12:6** – "We have different gifts, according to the grace given to each of us."

HOW TO BE A CHRISTIAN BUSINESS WOMAN

DO THE HARDEST THINGS FIRST

Doing the hardest things first saves time and energy. I used to dread working on attorney reports for patients and answering doctors' slandering reports against patients' injuries. It was arduous and time-consuming, and with no reimbursement, except that it was "the right thing to do." Reports and rebuttals typically were not appreciated by the patient, as they could not understand the time and mental energy involved for completion. I wasted time worrying about completing patient's paperwork.

Once I recognized that I needed to do the hardest thing on my "to-do" list first, stress diminished and I enjoyed the rest of the day in peace.

THERE IS A TIME TO BUILD AND A TIME TO SELL

If you are struggling with a decision about building or opening your business, God's business handbook tells us what to do – ask! God is not going to reprimand you for asking a question, for He is a great teacher.

> **James 1:5** – "But if anyone of you who lacks wisdom, let him ask of God, who gives to all generously and without reproach, and it will be given to him."

Your motivation to buy, sell, expand, open, and close should be based on truth, goodness, and Godly motivation. Do not make business decisions based on fear or greed.

In Ecclesiastes 3, God talks about a time to tear down before a time to build. Ladies, what does this mean for your life before starting your business?

PART ONE | STEP FOUR – PLANNING

> *Ecclesiastes 3:1-3*
> *"There is a time for everything, and a season to every activity*
> *under the heavens:*
> *A time to be born and a time to die,*
> *A time to plant and a time to uproot,*
> *A time to kill and a time to heal,*
> *A time to tear down and a time to build..."*

Business decisions motivated by fear keep your company in darkness. Sin and fear shrivel when brought into the light.

If one of your businesses is not producing, do not let your emotions rule a critical business decision. There is a time to tear down, and if you are emotionally invested and not looking at the truth, you will continue to lose money and prolong pain.

$$\text{Denial} + \text{Pain} = \text{Suffering.}$$

A closure and/or sell decision not made in a timely manner will result in throwing good money after bad. Make a decision, then the stress will subside; you will survive.

"Show me which way to go, for I entrust You with my life. Let the morning bring me word of your unfailing love, for I have put my trust in You. Show me the way I should go, for to You I lift up my soul" ***(Psalm 143:8)***. §

HOW TO BE A CHRISTIAN BUSINESS WOMAN

STEP FIVE

EMPLOYEES

While it may seem fair to honor everyone equally regardless of performance (everyone gets the Christmas ham), it is unwise. Giving everyone the same raise, in my opinion, is not correct.

So, how do we treat our employees? Honoring our employees is important. The employees who <u>have</u> worked the hardest and have done outstanding work should be called out and praised with financial incentives. The small percentage raise for everyone is fine, but not enough. Yes, we can empower all employees with a standard of living raise and a share in profitability, but empowering exceptional employees results in greater motivation and productivity in their work ***(Philippians 4:8)***.

> **Philippians 4:8** – "Finally, brothers and sisters, whatever is true, whatever is noble, whatever is right, whatever is pure, whatever is lovely, whatever is admirable – if anything is excellent or praiseworthy – think about such things."

HOW TO BE A CHRISTIAN BUSINESS WOMAN

In business, we cannot back down from every confrontation with every employee, or we will be eaten alive. Sometimes, employees do not value that which you value, but you are providing their paycheck and they are working for you. They do not pay you; you do not work for them. Employees have a responsibility to the business of which they work.

Hire employees who respect God, do not cheat, and have the potential skill set needed for the position.

WHINING EMPLOYEES

Whining employees can annoy you and pull down a Christian business. Delilah, the Philistine whom Samson loved, pestered him daily with her words. It annoyed his soul, and he gave up the secret behind the incredible strength with which God blessed him. Delilah exploited her lover, and so began Samson's demise.

I had an employee who whined daily, it seemed. The business was prospering, and a third location was opened. We needed her expertise in that location twenty minutes from our main office. This employee whined about the drive to the new location. Instead of telling her that she was fortunate to have a job and we appreciated her help, I did not speak the truth of my annoyance. I allowed myself to dread coming to work. However, she ultimately got a job in the same town twenty minutes away.

Speak your truth. Tell the employee, "I appreciate you, but you are annoying me. I feel you have a good job, and you are ungrateful."

A Christian businesswoman should speak the truth and not be hypersensitive. Being too sensitive can be destructive to your business dealings with your co-workers.

Do not be afraid to act with employees. Speaking truth immediately without injustice, but with righteousness and correction is important. The best time to correct an employee is when the negative action is

PART ONE | STEP FIVE – EMPLOYEES

occurring, not after less-than-optimal performance has become the norm.

> **Ephesians 4:15** – Instead, speaking the truth in love, we will grow to become in every respect the mature body of Him who is the head, that is, Christ.

You are the boss; be the boss. It is essential to provide correction, direction, and admonishment. Expect excellence from your employees. Christ calls us to excel and to rise above mediocrity, to be mature in every way, to become like Him.

We also should not be gullible with our employees. Your employees may feel entitled or falsely deserving, instead of appreciated. "A lie employees tell themselves to justify theft is, "It was my employer's fault for making it so easy to steal." Business owners are to render justice with grace.

For instance, in our first office, business was good, and the patients left happier, healthier, and straighter. The bank statement did not mirror the effort. I casually talked to my husband one night, and he checked the bank statement against the collections.

Unfortunately, we found out that the front desk assistant used $10,000 of accounts receivable as a down payment on a house for her family. She was given the option of returning the money or facing a theft charge. She somehow produced the "borrowed" money.

Be wise in your business. Put systems of audit and oversight in place at all levels of your business.

SPECIFICITY

You and your employees are all on the same team. It is good teamwork to assign specific duties to specific employees with specific deadlines. Delegate to a specific employee by name, give a time period, give a

HOW TO BE A CHRISTIAN BUSINESS WOMAN

budget, and give your expectation.

Lawyers, Lawsuits and Discretion

"I have told you these things, so that in Me you may have peace. In this world you will have trouble. But take heart. I have overcome the world" ***(John 16:33)***.

Christmas 2014 was tough for me. My husband and I were having trouble in our marriage, which is common if the priorities of family are not put above business. Even if you put your marriage first, business owners that are married can still have bumps on the road to business success.

I used to attend a Bible study taught by an attorney. I must have looked particularly haggard one Sunday, for he asked me to stay after class. In confidence, I explained that our marriage came to the point where my husband and I were choosing marriage over business. We had decided to sell three of our four offices to make the decision a reality.

My husband had contracts to sell two out of the three offices. The third office for sale was located where both the attorney and our clinic chiropractor lived. The female chiropractor was given the opportunity to buy the clinic, and if not, we wanted her to work in our main office. She ended up not purchasing the clinic, and to my surprise, one month after the birth of her baby, she sued me. My Bible instructor – AKA the attorney – represented the associate. The lawsuit was bogus in regards to pregnancy discrimination, but she used it as an outright lie to break a non-competition clause.

God's Word told me that the one who is taught the Word is to share all good things with the one who teaches him ***(Galatians 6:6)***. How could I? I had supper at his house with his wife and our entire Bible class, and now he chose to represent his client to sue me.

Galatians 6:6 – "Nevertheless, the one who receives instruction in the word should share all good things with their instructor."

PART ONE | STEP FIVE – EMPLOYEES

It was devastating. I viewed this associate more as a daughter than a colleague, and the break in confidence with my Bible instructor was a sensitive issue. I felt that he took my personal and confidential information to further his business as an attorney.

Furthermore, he was on the board at our church, and it was hurtful for me to go to church service and to look at him. I spoke of my discomfort to one of the pastors saying, "He is a bigwig in the church." The pastor answered, "God is the leader of this church, and there are different services." So, I got up earlier!

To protect yourself, especially in business and perhaps with personal issues, use discretion, even in a setting that could be assumed as "confidential."

God told me to turn the other cheek. Two years later, the lawsuit was settled, and the associate did not have to honor the non-competition clause.

Likewise, you may be sued by a customer, or an employee may feel that he or she has been wronged. My first civil court experience was when a patient hurt his neck, back, and shoulder in an automobile accident.

During one of the last treatments before his shoulder surgery, one of our clinic employees applied an electrical stimulation unit on the patient's skin. The unit left a blister on the patient. The patient's attorney called it a burn; I called it a blister. The patient ultimately settled with the help of his attorney for more than $52,000. The patient did not pay his chiropractic bill out of his settlement either, as it was more money in his pocket.

Instead of trusting God with the outcome, I worried, fretted, and did not sleep well for two years. This was detrimental to my health, my business, and my ability to function as a mother and as a wife. I looked on this patient as a father figure, and I did the absolute best job that I could have done for him. There was no gross malpractice; side effects can occur with medical care.

HOW TO BE A CHRISTIAN BUSINESS WOMAN

The motivation of this patient and his attorney was greed. I ultimately had to absorb the patient's bill. The only stipulation to settle was that they give a donation to a chiropractic association or a charity of their choice, a minimum amount of about $200.

> **Matthew 5:25** – "Settle matters quickly with your adversary who is taking you to court."

The judge stated that I should settle out of court and not take it to trial for the benefit of the reputation of our clinics. I settled out of fear. God does not want us to be foolish. He does not want us to be taken advantage of.

Cut your losses early. Malpractice cases, however, are grueling, and you may have troublesome dealings with attorneys. It is difficult to determine if you should stand up for what you feel is right versus the risk of going to public trial. The Bible does have something to say in regards to public trials. §

HOW TO BE A CHRISTIAN BUSINESS WOMAN

PART TWO

STEP SIX

HUSBANDS, BROTHERS, AND SISTERS

PRICILLA, A CHRISTIAN BUSINESSWOMAN

Your business may be just one aspect of your life in that you may be married to your business partner *(Acts 18:1-3, 2 Timothy 4:19)*. Richard Strauss, who speaks of married business partners in his book "Famous Couples if the Bible", writes that "When both business partners are aligned with God, their God-given resources can further God's kingdom."

We have a choice to further our kingdom with our business or God's kingdom with His plans for our business.

Aquila (the husband) and Pricilla (the wife) set up a business together in the ancient city of Corinth (south-central Greece) which made and sold tents. Their business prospered, and they needed a helping hand. God sent them a man named Paul. God used their business for His purpose, and soon, these business owners became believers in Christ Jesus.

HOW TO BE A CHRISTIAN BUSINESS WOMAN

Aquila and Pricilla soon opened up their home as a church and throughout their lives, continued helping other Christians, including a young speaker named Apollos.

SAPPHIRA, A CHRISTIAN BUSINESSWOMAN

There was another Christian husband-and-wife team called Ananias (husband) and Sapphira (wife) in the early church in Jerusalem. Sapphira had full knowledge and lied about a price Ananias, her husband, received for some land. Lying to herself, she may have used the cultural and societal excuse of "honoring her husband" *(Acts 5:1-13)*.

"Peter said to her, 'How could you agree to test the Spirit of the Lord? Look! The feet of the men who buried your husband are at the door, and they will carry you out also'" (Acts 5:9).

This is a great lesson for businesswomen who use our husbands as an excuse not to do the right thing. We will be responsible of what we have done. We cannot be passive when it suits us and hide behind our husbands.

"Wives, submit yourselves to your own husbands as you do to the Lord. For the husband is the head of the wife as Christ is the head of the church, His body, of which He is the Savior. Now as the church submits to Christ, so also wives should submit to their husbands in everything" (Ephesians 5:22-24).

If your husband or a partner is involved in your business and suggests or commands an action that is not within God's law, if it is not holy and good, then, you are not required to obey. Remember, God is your boss.

You cannot, in full knowledge, participate in an unrighteous act outside of God's will, and, in my opinion, that is not what the Bible teaches. God is your boss and your God; you must do what is right.

STEP SIX | HUSBANDS, BROTHERS, SISTERS

Do not simply agree with your husband or colleague when he is doing something wrong for your financial benefit. Do not gloss over sin for personal gain, or lie to the Holy Spirit about money. God is not fooled, and Sapphira paid with her life.

BROTHERS AND SISTERS

About five years ago in church, we passed around papers and promised to pray for each other. On these papers were struggles we were dealing with. The paper I received read, "Please pray for me, as I am struggling with sexual desire for a man in our church, but I am a married woman." I immediately judged this anonymous woman in my heart and said that would never happen to me…

Beware, you will be most tempted during the darkest times in your life.

The devil, Satan, waited until Jesus was starving, exhausted, and at the end of His trial. Be honest with yourself and your emotions. Do not put yourself into a situation that will be difficult for you to resist. You are human, and when dark thoughts come, acknowledge them like a cloud, and then let them pass. Pray to be led not into temptation, but to be delivered from the evil one *(Matthew 6:13)*.

Our culture emphasizes men's sexual drive and virility, but very little is said about women's sexual desire. However, it is a God-given gift, and it is perfectly normal. We just need to have boundaries and not step into a snare.

The best and easiest way to look at men in your business and professional life is to look at them as brothers. I love my brother, Mike; he is funny, kind, a great dad, and a good husband. I understand brothers.

As a woman, you have to deal with sexual desire, and attraction from others directed towards you. If you are in the service industry, this is referred to as transference, a psychological term.

HOW TO BE A CHRISTIAN BUSINESS WOMAN

If you do a good job for a patient or a client, they may interpret this to mean love or attraction. It is better to deal with this upfront; be honest and clear.

During a difficult time, two Christian brothers were kind to me. When going through tumultuous times, one is more open to sin, and it is common to misinterpret Christian brotherly kindness for something more. To deal with this, I handled it in an embarrassing way. After church one day, I just walked right up to the gentleman and told him that I could no longer talk to him or be around him due to feelings I was having for him. He looked at me with bizarre questioning and answered, "Betty, I have never felt that way about you at all."

I told my husband, and he laughed and said I was crazy. I asked him if he ever had similar feelings. He said, "Of course. I am married but I am not dead."

"No temptation has overtaken you except what is common to mankind. And God is faithful; He will not let you be tempted beyond what you can bear. But when you are tempted, He will also provide a way out so that you can endure it" ***(1 Corinthians 10:13-14)***.

In your business, you may have a time when you are the recipient of same-sex attraction as well. Once, a patient told me in confidence about her feelings. With uneasiness, I got my point across that I was married, I could not return her feelings, and that the doctor-patient relationship would have to end (I could not be her chiropractor) if her desires continued.

Clear boundaries are important. If your boundaries are crossed personally or professionally with customers, be courageous. Put truth above harmony.

STEP SEVEN

DO THE RIGHT THING

CORRUPTION

We, as Christian businesswomen, are called to glorify God, even when the economic system does not. So the question is, "How do Christian businesswomen run their businesses in a corrupt system?" The answer is to do what is right, no matter what it costs.

Consider and pray about your business and how your work and products reveal the glory of God.

HOW TO BE A CHRISTIAN BUSINESS WOMAN

Five Points That Can Help Us Follow God's Will & Word In Our Business

1. People must always be more important than products.
2. Keep away from pride in our own programs, plans, and successes.
3. Remember that God's will and word must never be compromised.
4. People must always be considered above the making of money.
5. Do what's right, no matter what it costs.
6. Be involved in businesses that provide worthwhile products or services, not just things that feed the world's desires.[3]

SLANDER AND COMPETITION

Eventually, you will face slander from your customers and from your employees. Employees may quit, sue you, steal from you, and they may badmouth you. You must astutely lay off, fire, reprimand, and admonish unruly workers for the health of your business. People have the capacity to stab you in the back, and we all can be nasty and hold grudges. God detests a person who stirs up conflict and strife **(Proverbs 6:16, 19)**.

Retaliating is uncomfortable for your clients and customers. As a Christian businesswomen, revenge and retaliation are not the image you want to project in your business. Your customers, suppliers, and

---

[3] The Life Application Study Bible New International Version Study Note
Notes and Bible Helps copyright ©1986 owned by assignment by Tyndale House Publishers, Inc.
Harmony of Gospels copyright ©1986 by James C. Galvin. All Rights reserved. Used by permission of Tyndale House Publishers, Inc

STEP SEVEN | DO THE RIGHT THING

competitors will not understand the Christian response of humility and gentleness in business, as these are not virtues valued in the business world.

When you are doing well, providing a good product or service, and having good employee output, the devil will not like it. When the attack comes, it may be a helpful sign for others watching you, that you are responding by "walking the walk."

Sometimes, suffering is God's will for you, but sometimes, it is the result of sin, with its consequences. At times, sin and persecution in business are people being mean and nasty or a consequence of what we have brought upon ourselves and our business.

I once interviewed a small business owner of a vintage country shop. This Christian businesswoman experienced cyber-bullying against her personally and against her business by an unknown user on her business Facebook page. The commenter had never been to her shop or purchased any goods on her site. I could feel her pain as she described the attack. When we own a business, we and want to protect our work.

When asked what this businesswomen did with the hurtful, unkind, and negative comments, she said, "I tried not to speak in corrupt speech in regards to this unknown woman. I did not retaliate." With great power and self control, the businesswoman demonstrated meekness.

Meekness is not weakness. John MacArthur, a pastor, explains, "Meekness is power under control."

Her customers went to her defense and commented on her business page that the critic had obviously never met the owner or been to her place of business. The unknown user promptly deleted her comments.

This Christian business owner went on to tell me that customers need to be treated with kindness and gentleness and we, as Christian businesswomen, should wear the garment of tenderheartedness. *"Therefore as God's chosen people, holy and dearly loved, clothe yourselves with compassion, kindness, humility, gentleness and patience"* ***(Colossians 3:12)***.

HOW TO BE A CHRISTIAN BUSINESS WOMAN

OPPOSITION

You will face opposition in your work and life. To overcome it, speak truth against it.

One of my favorite books in the Bible is the Book of Nehemiah; it is an impressive business book. Nehemiah is one of the men that God told to rebuild the torn-down wall of Jerusalem.

Nehemiah had the opposition of his own workers and the opposition of the rich and powerful within his own country. *"The next section was repaired by the men of Tekoa, but their nobles would not put their shoulders to the work under their supervisor"(Nehemiah 3:5).*

There was opposition from neighbors, other cultures, countries, and rulers against God's instruction to rebuild.

Nehemiah was mocked and despised, but he kept on *(Nehemiah 2:19)*. When you are mocked and despised, do not look down, look up!

Turning the other cheek does not mean that you blindly accept unfounded criticism and take it to heart. It does not mean that you hurt yourself, and it does not mean that you willingly hurt your business.

Nehemiah did not let the enemy come in and kill, destroy, and steal. He organized defensive strategies while continuing the work God had for him to do.

"I WANT IN THE FIGHT!"

Non-profit businesses are still businesses. In 2007, I spoke to the founder of the organization which became School Ministries Ohio. She recalled listening – twelve years earlier – to a "Focus on the Family" broadcast about religious freedom and was given a frightening insight: if something didn't change, her young children would be unable to freely express their faith in the public square. She prayed, "Lord, please put me in the fight. I don't care what battle. I want in." About

STEP SEVEN | DO THE RIGHT THING

a decade later, she was asked to lead her Ohio community's effort to reinstate a canceled released time Bible education program (where public school students can legally leave the public school with parental permission during school to study the Bible devotionally – at no cost to the public schools.) A few years after that, she started a statewide ministry to educate, equip and encourage the Body of Christ to start, maintain, and expand released time Bible programs all around Ohio.

She explained that to affect public policy, one must seek the Lord's will, think clearly, and prepare. She had to walk into battle relying on God's word and direction faithfully. She was given to understand that the people who held differing viewpoints were entitled to have their opinions heard – with understanding.

She prayed for, not against, those who had opposed released time, and recognized that there was an enemy, but he was not the community member who raised the issue or decision makers who canceled the program: *"For our struggle is not against flesh and blood but against the rulers, against the powers, against the world forces of this darkness, against the spiritual forces of wickedness in the heavenly places"* ***(Ephesians 6:12)***.

Takeaways? Treat those with whom you disagree with love and respect. If your work is anointed and ordained by God, it cannot be stopped. It is always better to be doing what God has called you to do, so before you begin, stop, pray, and be courageous. Then, go!

"Opponents must be gently instructed, in the hope that God will grant them repentance, leading them to a knowledge of the truth" ***(2 Timothy 2:25)***.

STEP EIGHT

ACT

Go for it! *"She considers a field and buys it; out of her earnings she plants a vineyard"* ***(Proverbs 31:16)***. Make decisions on what you can gain, not what you may lose. We honor God and worship God when we give our best and try our hardest.

God expects you to do your best. Sometimes, we are faced with difficult decisions that are in the gray area. Once, while browsing for Christmas, I placed a shiny, glitter-laden reindeer on the counter for purchase. His skinny long legs did not support his belly and the deer promptly shattered on the counter. Since I placed the plastic deer on counter, I utterly thought the "you break it, you buy it" rule applied. The business owner said no such thing, and she absorbed the loss. She chose the person in her customer over her product and profit on a purchase in a situation that was "gray." As the customer, my loyalty to this business resulted in a $25 gift certificate to each of my employees.

HOW TO BE A CHRISTIAN BUSINESS WOMAN

CLEAN HOUSE

Remember, He has given you the power of love and self-discipline. We have to take care of ourselves before we take a leadership role which means that we need to have strength and order in our own financial households before we can lead our homes, businesses, communities, and country.

In Jesus' day, in Jerusalem, the temple was in a state of chaos. *(Mark 11:15-16)*. Jesus did not want His Father's house to be an outdoor shopping mall. I laughed when our pastor explained the whips flying around, birds screaming, and money changers (bankers) getting reproached by Jesus.

> **Mark 11:15-16** – "On reaching Jerusalem, Jesus entered the temple courts and began driving out those who were buying and selling there. He overturned the tables of the money changers and the benches of those selling doves, and would not allow anyone to carry merchandise through the temple courts."

Jesus wants us to know that we need to have a clean house. Sometimes, employees lose a good attitude and despite attempts at correction, they feel entitled or stuck.

Cleaning house in your business may mean reviewing employees that do not fit the position or get the job done.

It is also important to keep your warehouses and offices physically clean, which takes a lot of work and energy.

Building a business is exhausting, but there is also labor involved in closing a business. Cleaning up your mess, other people's messes, your employees' messes, your customers' messes, and corporate messes can be difficult. The clean-up cost brings us to the foot of the Cross, recognizing how He suffered cleaning up our messes.

STEP EIGHT | ACT

"Then the governor's soldiers took Jesus into the Praetorium and gathered the whole company of soldiers around Him. They stripped Him and put a scarlet robe on Him, and then twisted together a crown of thorns and set it on His head. They put a staff in His right hand. Then, they knelt in front of Him and mocked Him. "Hail, King of the Jews!" they said. They spit on Him, and took the staff and struck Him on the head again and again" **(Matthew 27-30)**.

BE STRONG AND COURAGEOUS

Jesus has a lot to say about bullies. We are not to take revenge, because revenge is the Lord's. Turning the other cheek does not mean that we do not speak. When Jesus was slapped, He spoke the truth. "If I said something wrong," Jesus replied, *"testify as to what is wrong. But if I spoke the truth, why did you strike me?"* **(John 18:23)**.

Be truthful; what is the worst that can happen? **(Romans 8:31)**

> **Romans 8:31** – "...If God is for us, who can be against us?"

My grandmother was born and raised in the small town of Tabor, South Dakota. Every Christmas, Tabor had Christmas Mass in the Bohemian language. It was one of the most beautiful experiences I have had, and as a child, I was so grateful to be there worshiping God.

A great Jewish leader spent time working at a mountain called Tabor. Deborah was a leader in the country of Israel.

There was a time when the Jews did not want to follow their God. So, He gave them into the hands of another king named Jabin. King Jabin had the greatest military armament of the time. King Jabin was the leader of the country called Canaan.

Jabin was a cruel king, and after two decades, God's people, the Israelites, cried out.

HOW TO BE A CHRISTIAN BUSINESS WOMAN

Israel's leader, Deborah, told her general that God commanded him to take 10,000 men and head up to Mount Tabor and fight. General Barak said, "No way, unless you come with me."

Deborah replied, "Okay, General Barak, but the victory will go to someone different – a lady!"

"'Certainly,' Deborah said, 'I will go with you. But because of the course you are taking, the honor will not be yours, for the Lord will deliver Sisera into the hands of a woman.' So Deborah went with Barak to Kedesh" *(Judges 4:9)*.

What Is Canaan?

Canaan was the name of a large, prosperous country (at times independent, at others a tributary to Egypt) which corresponds roughly to present-day Lebanon, Syria, and Israel and was also known as Phoenicia.

The courageous victor Deborah was describing a housewife named Jael.

"But Jael, Heber's wife, picked up a tent peg and a hammer and went quietly to him while he lay fast asleep, exhausted. She drove the peg through his temple into the ground, and he died" *(Judges 4:21)*.

Country	Leaders	Generals	Armament
Israel	Deborah (Prophetess)	Barak	God & 10,000 men
Canaan	Jabin (King)	Sisera	An expertly trained army and 900 chariots fitted with iron

STEP EIGHT | ACT

Deborah wanted to serve God. She did not deny or resist her position in her culture as a woman and a wife, but she never allowed herself to be hindered by it either. Women have strength in connecting with others as well as the strength to lead.

Ladies, be courageous leaders! Be like Deborah!

Jael was a housewife who God saw and gave the strength to be successful and courageous. You also possess business attributes from the running of your home. You are highly valued and capable of the financial health of your family, utilizing the resources of food, clothing, shelter, and time.

Ladies, be strong! Emulate Jael! Act!

I'll admit that I never liked our first chiropractic business location. Except for the patients, it was scary. Drug dealers lived behind the clinic. I would decorate the front yard to make it look nice for the patients, and the very next day, harvest pumpkins would be smashed. In business, it is good to protect yourself; I kept a gun in a lock box under my desk. Christian Businesswoman have the responsibility to protect ourselves, our employees, and our businesses.

"He said to them, 'But now if you have a purse, take it, and also a bag; and if you do not have a sword, sell your cloak and buy one'" *(Luke 22:36).*

BUSINESS OPPORTUNITIES AND FAMILY

Multiple decisions will come up daily as a business owner. It is your job to make the best decision. As a female business owner, you may have more than one business. The family, another type of business, can be looked upon as logistics (getting children to and from activities), and financial management.

When my daughter was in the fourth grade, she was not getting enough rest. The school called and said that she had a migraine. The clinic, at

HOW TO BE A CHRISTIAN BUSINESS WOMAN

the time, was full of patients having headaches and ailments, such as sciatic and disc injuries and my husband was out of town.

Putting business first, I finished with all of the patients and then went to pick her up. It was not an emergency, and she was fine. However, I felt like I should have tended to my daughter earlier. Another time, my son was playing soccer in high school and had heat exhaustion. Again, the clinic was full of patients, so I finished with them first. I chose unwisely a second time and ended up meeting my husband and my son in the emergency room.

I did not have my priorities in order. Similarly, you will make mistakes, and you will continue to make them again until you learn; keep trying. *"And forgive us our debts as we also have forgiven our debtors"* **(Matthew 6:12)**. Ask God for forgiveness, then forgive yourself.

For years, my priorities were out of alignment, which made decisions stressful. Take time to make your priority list so when emergencies and daily "fires" come up, the decision is already made.

STORMS

Whatever mistakes you make may become storms. Remember, God is in charge, and your perceived mistakes will ultimately result in divine purpose. If you serve God and go the extra mile, you do not automatically get good kids, a great marriage, and a new car. That is not how it works. In actuality, you may find that you get sick, your dog dies, and you lose your house.

Serving God may or may not result in blessings seen immediately on this side of Heaven, but God is the God who sees. *"She gave this name to the Lord who spoke to her 'You are the God who sees me,' for she said, 'I have now seen the One who sees me'"* **(Genesis 16:13)**. Your business will not always be peaceful or calm.

God is good, so why would He allow us to undergo trials, storms, and hurricanes?

STEP EIGHT | ACT

Because He loves us, our Father disciplines His children for purification. He does this for our own good, and admittedly, it is painful. *"No discipline seems pleasant at the time, but painful. Later on, however, it produces a harvest of righteousness and peace for those who have been trained by it"* **(Hebrews 12:11)**.

PRODUCTIVE PAIN

In February 2015, I started having pain walking around our local reservoir. Then, it progressed to not being able to align patients. I diagnosed myself with infrapatellar tendinosis (the tendon at the bottom of the kneecap wearing down) and went to an orthopedic surgeon.

He administered a cortisone shot, and it was a miracle for one day. I could run again. Wow! Two days later, it was not better, so after a week, I called and asked the surgeon if he would order an MRI.

The MRI came back positive for neoplasm (a tumor), so he ordered a stat MRI, which was diagnosed as cancer. The radiologist was kind enough to talk to me and gave me a paper with the words "synovial sarcoma." Then, he laughed nervously and wished me good luck. I got three other radiologists' opinions and they concurred.

Synovial sarcomas are deadly, body-eating cancers. Wow – a death sentence at 46. Synovial sarcomas over five centimeters have a 50 percent survival rate at five years. Mine was two centimeters, so I was looking at a 90 percent survival rate at five years. I remember crying and being crushed, believing that I would not get to see my kids marry or meet my grandchildren.

The first three weeks were incredibly busy getting tests and records. A terminal diagnosis is like getting slammed by an ocean wave. It feels like your head gets whiplash.

Finally, I was sent to a musculoskeletal orthopedic oncologist.

HOW TO BE A CHRISTIAN BUSINESS WOMAN

There was hope…he told me it may be a giant cell tumor (a noncancerous growth).

What – I may live? The chaotic storm that I thought would claim my life might be calmed soon? A painful biopsy a week later confirmed it. *"Come and see, all who fear God, and what God has done, His awesome deed for mankind"* ***(Psalm 66:5)***.

God had whispered to my soul about two months before this happened that I would live to be an old woman. The original diagnosis did not make sense – a 46-year-old lady with a childhood disease of osteosarcoma of the knee. Instead of trusting God, I trusted in man's word. However, God's grace prevailed. God used my pain and disbelief of His answer, as a way to help me understand what patients, friends, and family begin to suffer at the time of a medical diagnosis.

"And the God of all grace, who called you to His eternal glory in Christ, after you have suffered a little while, will Himself restore you and make you strong, firm, and steadfast" ***(1 Peter 5:10)***.

STEP NINE

BEING A BUSINESS<u>WOMAN</u>

There is an non-biblical teaching, due partly to patriarchy and cultural-ism, that businesswomen are to accept sexual innuendos. Degradation about business success may accompany inappropriate attributes to physical appearance. Women are to be clothed in dignity. You can be a business owner and still be a woman.

Most women, I believe, have certain gender-based disadvantages in business. We have to learn quickly not to "take everything to heart." Women are different from men both emotionally and physically. Different seasons in our lives can play dramatic roles in our business production. Protecting your heart will be of utmost importance ***(Proverbs 4:23)***. A counselor once told me to have a guard around my heart like a door. Open it up to let love out, but keep it closed, and do not let destructive arrows in.

Proverbs 4:23 – "Above all else, guard your heart, for everything you do flows from it."

HOW TO BE A CHRISTIAN BUSINESS WOMAN

Oswald Chambers understood irritations and not letting them misdirect purpose. The strenuous, demanding, and grueling nature of daily business decisions and dealing with a variety of personalities can be unhealthy. In his book, "Abandoned to God: The Life Story of The Author of My Utmost for His Highest," he wrote a letter to a friend going through a storm:

> "Praise God for your report that the devil is paying attention to you – so long as he keeps firing at us, you may depend he thinks that we are worth watching. My hearty greeting to your wife and bairns (kids). The "plague of flies" was not peculiar to Egypt – you will find them in the shape of busy little people that try to get over the window of your soul and irritate your outlook. God bless you."
>
> Yours,
>
> Oswald Chambers

EMOTIONS

Being overly sensitive does not portray strength and can be detrimental to your business. Grigsby and Cobb warn us in the book, "The Politically Incorrect Wife,":

> "We don't want our emotions to be controlled by others. Don't be so sensitive that you let your feelings and emotions be set by another's treatment of you. Jesus didn't do that. He continued to live His life with honor, dignity, love and mercy through the most difficult times. Don't be judgmental or unfriendly. Don't allow yourself to be too easily wounded, crushed, or hurt. Guard against bitterness and be quick to forgive. Ask Jesus to help develop these attitudes in you when you face challenging times."

STEP NINE | BEING A BUSINES<u>WOMAN</u>

Unfortunately, women are more likely to cry than men. I was asked to give a blessing in our county for the Annual Pastor's Gathering to bless our town. I was a representative for the healthcare community. Emotions ran high that day as my business partner/husband and I had a disagreement earlier that day. I did not think he would show up, but he surprised me. I blubbered for about two minutes and could not stop. As it was more than a little cry, I could not talk and mouthed to my pastor and friends to pray for me.

What someone does and says means nothing about you.

Crying was not effective for the talk; I could not get my thoughts out. I wasted the pastors' time, and I was never asked back, (I do not blame them).

Take a few breaths if your emotions are running high. If you are overly sensitive, you will not be productive to your business or community. Emotions are not wrong, but they need to be expressed at the correct times and in the correct settings.

MULTITASKING

Women can be skilled in multitasking, but multitasking can also be inefficient and stressful. It is better to concentrate on one task at a time. When running a business, there are many greedy agendas pulling on your time. Before you go into a room, if there are too many fires, stop, refocus, clear your mind, concentrate, and then, proceed.

ANGER

A woman I interviewed said this: "Men and women react differently to anger. Anger does not typically bother most men and at times, can

HOW TO BE A CHRISTIAN BUSINESS WOMAN

empower them. Women back away from other's expression of anger."

The leading cause of death for women is now heart disease; anger, in my opinion, is the contributing factor. Businesswomen go to battle daily. Usually when angry, we take perceived insults as personal affronts.

Jesus experienced anger, but His was a righteous anger about right and wrong. Usually, our anger is about pride. *"Fools give full vent to their rage, but the wise bring calm in the end"* **(Proverbs 29:11)**.

ENVY

Other people may envy you without understanding how much work, time, and investment take place in a business operation. Owning your own business is a whole different lifestyle.

Envy is unattainable excellence and jealousy towards others.

In reality, if you are not a business owner, it is difficult to understand. A business owner is a different entity than an employee. An employee can go home and not worry when they are off the clock. A business owner is never off the clock; her business is like her baby.

You may also encounter jealousy and envy toward others. This usually happens in your own profession or work group. For instance, a hairdresser is not normally jealous of and does not envy an excellent shoe salesman.

Envy can be greed in disguise. We want what other people have, but we realize and learn that God gave them specific talents for His will to help His people in creation.

When we start getting out of God's will and chasing others' talents and gifts, it will cause heartache. Even though I have a DC, FACO,

STEP NINE | BEING A BUSINES<u>WOMAN</u>

FIAMA, and CCSP which is an extra 15 initials behind my name, I used to struggle terribly with envy to my detriment. I could not overcome this wretched sin in my own power, so I asked God for help.

STOP WHINING

One night, my husband and I were at the dinner table, and I was whining about my day at work. Soon I heard, *"God lives inside of you; act like it!"* *"Do everything without grumbling or arguing"* **(Philippians 2:14)**.

WITCHY WITH A "B"

Principals, CEOs, and female managers do not have to threaten or demean to do their job. You have power. This is especially difficult for women who hold higher positions than men. Men and women will test your authority. Acknowledge their attempts and let it pass or send it back with a bit of humor. Do not be the witch abusing your authority; just be confident.

HOW DO WOMEN DEMAND RESPECT?

Deborah commanded respect through good leadership. She demonstrated what we as women can accomplish when God is in control. We are not being disrespectful to men, whether they be business partners, husbands, or our customers, just because they do not like the answer. We are not wrong if we are speaking truth.

HOW TO BE A CHRISTIAN BUSINESS WOMAN

GO HIDE

A woman in our church was on a prayer committee to build a new church at our current location. When I asked her about how the process progressed, she said, "When we were planning and praying for what God wanted for

What is a rampart?
A defensive wall of a castle or a walled city having a broad top with a walkway.

His congregation, it was like someone was undermining and knew where it would hurt each individual member of the committee the most personally and professionally." When the wolves are attacking, it is okay to hide.

> **Matthew 14:23** – "After He had dismissed them, He went up on a mountainside by Himself to pray. Later that night, He was there alone."

When family and business responsibilities are too painful, and you are at the end of your rope, simply go hide under His shadow. *"He will cover you with His feathers and under His wings you will find refuge, His faithfulness will be your shield and rampart"* **(Psalm 91:4)**.

Sometimes we all need to get away from people. Renew, restore, then, get back in the game. "Stay-cations" do not work. Women understand that there is more work at home than at work. Jesus went away often to rest, renew and restore *(Matthew 14:23)*.

We can get away, too, and we should.

When you have worked hard helping people and serving, remember that God is not unjust. He sees your service. He will not forget your work and the love you have shown Him as you have helped His people and continue to help them. *"May the Lord reward your work, and your wages be full from the Lord, the God of Israel, under whose wings you have come to seek refuge"* **(Ruth 2:12)**.

STEP NINE | BEING A BUSINESS<u>WOMAN</u>

Once while getting my nails done, I asked the female manicurist with five kids and a husband at home what was the hardest part of her work. She said that she has nothing left when she goes home. Dealing with customers made her physically and mentally exhausted. Women are givers, but if we empty our cups completely, we have nothing left for our children and husbands.

What is a Selah?
Selah means pause, think about it.

When you have nothing left to give, put your mind back on Him, not on your problems or your business. "Be still." Just be in the sweet spot of His grace and His presence. During your needed precious time with God you do not have to be anywhere, fix anything, or do anything. "He says, *'Be still and know that I am God. I will be exalted among the nations, I will be exalted in the earth.' Selah*" **(Psalm 46:10)**. Go exalt Him!

Then, because so many people were coming and going that they did not even have a chance to eat, He said to them, 'Come with Me by yourselves to a quiet place and get some rest' " **(Mark 6:31)**. It is tremendous work to have your own business. You will need much rest.

STEP TEN

THANKFULNESS

BUILD, DO NOT DESTROY

Wise women build their homes and do not destroy them with their own hands. Your home includes much more than four walls – it is your body, spirit, family, and business. You have the greatest power to build your business, but also to destroy all you have built. To prevent self destruction, practice gratitude.

Be thankful with your success by continued learning, planning, and investing in your company and your talents. Develop a strong desire to learn and to grow so you can help more people with your business and products.

My husband and I rented a house for years while we built up our little two-room natural healthcare business. We did not have a TV, and when our family wanted to watch a movie, we would go back to the clinic and all sit on a little bench. We did not build or buy a house. First, we built our business. *(Proverbs 24:27)*.

HOW TO BE A CHRISTIAN BUSINESS WOMAN

> **Proverbs 24:27** – "Put your outdoor work in order and get your fields ready; after that, build your house."

I saw this concept in a young Christian man at our church. Before he would walk down the aisle, he got a job and rented a house.

I remember coming home after attending seminars. The house was a mess. The children wanted my attention, so they were fighting. After I had been at a seminar all weekend, my husband and the children would be expecting supper. My husband would be sitting on the couch, watching TV, overwhelmed, and under-appreciated.

Likewise you will, feel overwhelmed and under-appreciated. When you have business and work responsibilities, but also have a family, it is normal not to be thanked; it is common to be under-appreciated. Only one out of ten people, including your family, may thank you.

You have a 1 in 10 chance of being thanked!

Jesus had this experience after healing a group of men with a flesh-eating condition called leprosy. *"Then Jesus asked, 'Were not all ten cleansed? Where are the other nine?'"* **(Luke 17:17)**.

WHAT TO DO WITH ABUNDANCE?

When your abundance, your passion, and purpose align with God's word, there will be success and overflowing blessing. Women helped bankroll Jesus' ministry.

"After this, Jesus traveled about from one town and village to another, proclaiming the good news of the kingdom of God. The Twelve were with him, and also some women who had been cured of evil spirits and diseases: Mary (called Magdelene) from whom seven demons had come out; Joanna the wife of Chuza, the manager of Herod's

PART TWO | FINANCIAL DATA

household; Susanna; and many others. These women were helping to support them out of their own means." **(Luke 8:1-3)**

Here, the Bible very clearly discusses our obligation to give with cheerful hearts to our brothers and sisters of our faith.

"Therefore, as we have the opportunity, let us do good to all people, especially to those who belong to the family of believers" **(Galatians 6:10)**.

THANKFULNESS

Astonishingly, Jesus thanked God before He went to the cross, despite knowing the torture that He would soon endure. *"And He took bread, gave thanks and broke it, and gave it to them, saying, 'This is My body given for you; do this in remembrance of Me"* **(Luke 22:19)**.

As a little country girl from North Dakota, I could not have imagined such an incredible life, nor planned it myself.

I am exceedingly thankful for Jesus' gift, dream, and purpose that my business holds in God's kingdom, here on His planet Earth.

My husband gave up his career as a design engineer and was instrumental in helping our business succeed – a Navy man, with integrity, who put aside his career desires and aspirations to help his wife succeed. For this, I will always be grateful.

I am also thankful for our children; our beloved son, John, and our beautiful daughter Catherine. I think of you both with great joy.

With gratitude for their assistance, the editors, trasnscriptionists, and designers who made this book the best it could be.

I am also grateful to all employees that I have had the honor to help serve with, and finally I thank all the patients that the good Lord has let me share a small part of their lives.

A FINAL THOUGHT

PARTING BLESSING

It has been my joy to be able to help you and your business in a small way, and I pray that your hearts will be flooded with light so that you can understand the confident hope of His calling to your life and your business, for He loves His people.

– Betty

HOW TO BE A CHRISTIAN BUSINESS WOMAN

Sample Business Plan

Cover Sheet

1. Identify the business.
2. Identify the location, phone number, or where the principles can be reached.
3. Identify who the plan is to be submitted to.
4. Identify who prepared the plan.

Statement of Purpose

1. Who is asking for money?
2. What is the business structure? (i.e. sole proprietorship, partnership, corporation, sub chapter S Corp, or Limited Liability Company)
3. How much money?
4. What is the money for?
5. How will the funds benefit the business?
6. Why does the loan or investment make sense?
7. How will the fund be repaid?

Table of Contents

I. Part One | The Business
II. Part Two | Financial Data
III. Part Three | Supporting Documents

SAMPLE BUSINESS PLAN

Part One | The Business

Description of Business

1. Type of Business (i.e. merchandising, manufacturing, or service)
2. Status of Business (startup, expansion, etc.)
3. Form of Business (sole proprietorship, partnership, or corporation)
4. Why will the business be profitable?
5. When will your business begin operations?
6. What are the business hours and days of regular operations?
7. If seasonal, or if the hours will be adjusted seasonally.
8. Why will you be successful in the business?
9. What is your experience in the business?
10. Have you discussed the business with possible competitors?
11. What will be special about your business?
12. Will trade suppliers provide any managerial or technical support?
13. Have you asked about trade credit terms?
14. What credit terms will you extend to customers?
15. Do you have any contracts or letters of intent?

The Market

1. Who is your market?
2. What is the present size of the market?

HOW TO BE A CHRISTIAN BUSINESS WOMAN

3. What percent of the market will you have?
4. What is the market's growth potential?
5. As the market grows, does your share of the market decrease?
6. How are you going to satisfy your market?
7. How will you price your service or product to ensure a fair profit and be competitive?
8. How will you attract and keep the market? (Advertising, radio, and TV)
9. How can you expand your market?
10. If premium price, what justifies the premium?

Competition

1. Who are your five nearest competitors?
2. How will your operation be better than the competition?
3. How is the competition's business: steady, increasing, decreasing, and why?
4. What is the competition's strengths and weaknesses?
5. How is the competition the same or different from you?
6. Did you learn anything from how the competition operates?

Location of The Business

1. What is the business address?
2. Describe the physical features of the building?
3. Lease or own? – Terms of the lease.
4. Identify renovations and costs.

SAMPLE BUSINESS PLAN

Location Of The Business Continued...

5. Zoning.
6. What other business are in the area?
7. Why is this the right place to start?
8. Effect of the location on operating costs.

Management

1. Personal history of principles, including financial statements.
2. Work experience related to the business.
3. Assignment of responsibilities and duties.
4. Salaries.
5. Resources available to the business (consultants, legal, accounting, marketing, business information centers, economic development groups).

Personnel

1. What are the personnel needs at start-up: in year one, year two, and year three?
2. What skills are required?
3. Are the skills available – Who will train the unskilled?
4. Employment – full time or part time?
5. Salary or wages?
6. Fringe benefits?
7. Overtime?

HOW TO BE A CHRISTIAN BUSINESS WOMAN

Application & Requirements of Loans

1. How is the loan to be spent? (working capital, equipment, inventory, supplies)
2. What are the items to be bought? (names and models)
3. Who is the supplier? – Quote when possible.
4. What is the price?
5. Are there additional charges: use tax, installation, freight, controls, etc?
6. How will the loan increase your profits?

Summary

In a brief statement, summarize all of the above statements.

Part 2 | Financial Data

Sources and Applications of Funding

1. List sources of securing capital (i.e. mortgage loan, term loan, line of credit, investment, etc).
2. List major categories of expenditures (real prop, equipment, remodeling costs, inventory, working capital, contingency reserve).

Capital Equipment List

1. As a minimum, the listing would show: description of equipment; type or model number; cost, including tax, freight, and installation.
2. Secure prices from suppliers.

SAMPLE BUSINESS PLAN

Income and Cash Flow Forecasting

1. Both forecasts should be prepared for two years in advance.[4]

2. Forecast first year on a month-by-month basis. If no profit is shown in the first year, continue projection by month until a profit is shown and then record quarterly.

Part 3 | Supporting Documents

Required Documents

1. Resumes

2. Quotes or estimates from suppliers

3. References or letters of support from credible people who know you

Desirable Documents

1. Credit information – Personal Credit

2. Letters of intent from prospective customers

3. Leases or rental requirements

4. Legal documents pertaining to the business

5. Marketing data – demographics, etc

6. Physical layout of business space

---

[4] Sample Business Plan (1997)
Small Business Administration

APPENDIX

BUSINESS ADVICE

Proverbs 31:18 "She sees that her trading is profitable, and her lamp does not go out at night."

Jeremiah 8:4 "Say to them, 'This is what is the Lord says: 'When people fall down, do they not get up?'"

DIRECTION

Genesis 9:7 "As for you, be fruitful and increase in number; multiply on the earth and increase upon it."

Proverbs 3:5-6 "Trust in the Lord with all your heart and lean not on your own understanding. In all your ways, submit to Him, and He will make your paths straight."

Ephesians 4:15 "Instead, speaking the truth in love, we will grow to become in every respect the mature body of Him who is the head, that is, Christ."

Matthew 10:16 "I am sending you out like sheep among wolves. Therefore, be as shrewd as snakes and as innocent as doves."

Proverbs 15:22 "Plans fail for lack of counsel, but with many advisers, they succeed."

1 Thessalonians 5:8 "But since we belong to the day, let us be sober, putting on faith and love as a breastplate, and the hope of salvation as a helmet."

Philippians 4:8 "Finally, brothers, whatever is true, whatever is noble, whatever is right, whatever is pure, whatever is lovely, whatever is admirable – if anything is excellent or praiseworthy – think about such things."

APPENDIX

WISDOM

Luke 12:15 "Then He said to them, "Watch out! Be on your guard against all kinds of greed; life does not consist in an abundance of possessions."

Proverbs 28:20 "A faithful person will be richly blessed, but one eager to get rich will not go unpunished."

Luke 18:41 "What do you want me to do for you?" "Lord, I want to see," he replied.

Proverbs 14:30 "A heart at peace gives life to the body, but envy rots the bones."

Romans 1:20 "For since the creation of the world, God's invisible qualities – His eternal power and divine nature – have been clearly seen, being understood from what has been made, so that men are without excuse."

Revelations 18:3 "For all the nations have drunk the maddening wine of her adulteries. The kings of the earth committed adultery with her, and the merchants of the earth grew rich from her excessive luxuries."

Revelations 18:15 "The merchants who sold these things and gained their wealth from her will stand far off, terrified at her torment. They will weep and mourn."

Job 17:9 "Nevertheless, the righteous will hold to their ways, and those with clean hands will grow stronger."

Isaiah 55:9 "As the heavens are higher than the earth, so are My ways higher than your ways and My thoughts than your thoughts."

1 Timothy 4:4 "For everything God created is good, and nothing is to be rejected if it is received with thanksgiving."

APPENDIX

WISDOM (CONT.)

Proverbs 1:7 "The fear of the Lord is the beginning of knowledge, but fools despise wisdom and instruction."

Ecclesiastes 5:12 "The sleep of a laborer is sweet, whether they eat little or much, but the abundance of a rich man permits him no sleep."

Hebrews 12:11 "No discipline seems pleasant at the time, but painful. Later on, however, it produces a harvest of righteousness and peace for those who have been trained by it."

Matthew 17:5 "While He was still speaking, a bright cloud covered them, and a voice from the cloud said, 'This is my Son, whom I love; with Him I am well pleased. Listen to Him!'"

Proverbs 25:10 "Or the one who hears it may shame you and the charge against you will stand."

POWER

2 Timothy 1:7 "For the spirit God gave us does not make us timid, but gives us power, love, and self-discipline."

1 Peter 3:6 "Like Sarah, who obeyed Abraham and called him her lord. You are her daughters if you do what is right and do not give way to fear."

PROTECTION

Psalm 91:4 "He will cover you with His feathers, and under His wings you will find refuge; His faithfulness will be your shield and your rampart."

Psalm 34:8 "Taste and see that the Lord is good; blessed is the one who takes refuge in Him."

APPENDIX

FAILURE

Proverbs 24:16 "For though the righteous fall seven times, they rise again, but the wicked stumble when calamity strikes."

Psalm 119:71 "It was good for me to be afflicted that I might learn your decrees."

Lamentations 3:39 "Why should the living complain when punished for their sins?"

SUPPLIES

2 Corinthians 9:10 "Now He who supplies seed to the sower and bread for food will also supply and increase your store of seed and enlarge the harvest of your righteousness."

MISTAKES

Proverbs 26:11 "As a dog returns to its vomit, so fools repeat their folly."

Romans 7:19 "For I do not do the good I want to do, but the evil I do not want to do – this I keep on doing."

GUIDANCE

Psalm 37:23 "The Lord makes firm the steps of one who delights in Him."

James 4:17 "If anyone, then, knows the good they ought to do and doesn't do it, it is a sin for them."

Acts 10:38 "How God anointed Jesus of Nazareth with the Holy Spirit and power, and how He went around doing good and healing all who were under the power of the devil, because God was with Him."

APPENDIX

GUIDANCE (CONT.)

Proverbs 16:3 "Commit to the Lord whatever you do, and He will establish your plans."

Proverbs 16:9 "In their hearts, humans plan their course, but the Lord establishes their steps."

Proverbs 31:13 "She selects wool and flax and works with eager hands."

Proverbs 31:27 "She watches over the affairs of her household and does not eat the bread of idleness."

Proverbs 4:23 "Above all else, guard your heart, for everything you do flows from it."

Exodus 18:21 "But select capable men from all the people – men who fear God, trustworthy men who hate dishonest gain and appoint them as officials over thousands, hundreds, fifties, and tens."

Matthew 7:6 "Do not give dogs what is sacred; do not throw your pearls to pigs. If you do, they may trample them under their feet, and then turn and tear you to pieces."

Leviticus 19:15 "Do not pervert justice; do not show partiality to the poor or favoritism to the great, but judge your neighbor fairly."

ACTION

Proverbs 31:16 "She considers a field and buys it; out of her earnings, she plants a vineyard."

Proverbs 24:27 "Put your outdoor work in order and get your fields ready; after that, build your house."

APPENDIX

Luke 22:36 He said to them, "But now if you have a purse, take it, and also a bag; and if you don't have a sword, swell your cloak, and buy one."

Psalm 46:10 He says, "Be still, and know that I am God; I will be exalted among the nations, I will be exalted in the earth."

Philippians 3:14 "I press on toward the goal to win the prize for which God has called me heavenward in Christ Jesus."

Isaiah 43:18 "Forget the former things; do not dwell on the past."

Hebrews 12:12 "Therefore, strengthen your feeble arms and weak knees."

Luke 6:38 "Give, and it will be given to you. A good measure, pressed down, shaken together, and running over, will be poured into your lap. For with the measure you use, it will be measured to you."

Proverbs 3:27 "Do not withhold good from those to whom it is due, when it is in your power to act."

Matthew 5:48 "Be perfect, therefore, as you heavenly Father is perfect."

Judges 4:21 "But Jael, Heber's wife, picked up a tent peg and a hammer and went quietly to him while he lay fast asleep, exhausted. She drove the peg through his temple into the ground, and he died."

CONFLICT

Proverbs 25:21 "If your enemy is hungry, give him food to eat; if he is thirsty, give him water to drink."

Proverbs 26:21 "As charcoal to embers and as wood to fire, so is the quarrelsome person for kindling strife."

APPENDIX

CONFLICT (CONT.)

Ephesians 4:14 "Then, we will no longer be infants, tossed back and forth by the waves, and blown here and there by every wind of teaching and by the cunning and craftiness of people in their deceitful scheming."

2 Corinthians 4:8-9 "We are hard pressed on every side but not crushed: perplexed, but not in despair; persecuted, but not abandoned; struck down, but not destroyed."

Mark 11:15 "On reaching Jerusalem, Jesus entered the temple area and began driving out those who were buying and selling there. He overturned the tables of the money changers and the benches of those selling doves."

Proverbs 25:9 "If you take your neighbor to court, do not betray another's confidence."

2 Chronicles 20:15 "He said, 'Listen, King Jehoshaphat and all who live in Judah and Jerusalem! This is what the Lord says to you: 'Do not be afraid or discouraged because of this vast army. For the battle is not yours, but God's.'"

Exodus 14:14 "The Lord will fight for you; you need only to be still."

GREED

Ecclesiastes 7:7 "Extortion turns a wise man into a fool, and a bribe corrupts the heart."

Isaiah 5:9 "The Lord Almighty has declared in my hearing: 'Surely the great houses will become desolate, the fine mansions left without occupants.'"

Proverbs 23:4 "Do not wear yourself out to get rich; do not trust your own cleverness."

APPENDIX

Proverbs 11:6 "The righteousness of the upright delivers them, but the unfaithful are trapped by evil desires."

Proverbs 28:20 "A faithful man will be richly blessed, but one eager to get rich will not go unpunished."

Proverbs 13:11 "Dishonest money dwindles away, but whoever gathers money little by little makes it grow."

Proverbs 11:1 "The Lord detests dishonest scales, but accurate weights find favor with Him."

OWNERSHIP

Proverbs 19:21 "Many are the plans in a person's heart, but it is the Lord's purpose that prevails."

Isaiah 45:7 "I form the light and create darkness; I bring prosperity and create disaster; I, the Lord, do all these things."

Isaiah 45:9 "Woe to those that quarrel with their Maker, those who are nothing but potsherds among the potsherds on the ground. Does the clay say to the potter, 'What are you making?' Does your work say, "The potter has no hands?'"

Psalm 24:1 "The earth is the Lord's, and everything in it, the world and all who live in it."

PERSEVERANCE

Joshua 23:14 "Now I am about to go the way of all the earth. You know with all your heart and soul that not one of all the good promises the Lord, your God, gave you has failed. Every promise has been fulfilled; not one has failed."

Hebrews 12:4 "In your struggle against sin, you have not yet resisted to the point of shedding your blood."

APPENDIX

PERSEVERANCE (CONT.)

Hebrews 12:5 "And have you completely forgotten this word of encouragement that addresses you as a father addresses his son: It says, 'My son, do not make light of the Lord's discipline, and do not lose heart when He rebukes you.'"

Hebrews 12:6 "Because the Lord disciplines the one He loves, and He chastens everyone He accepts as His son."

Hebrews 12:7 "Endure hardship as discipline; God is treating you as His children. For what children are not disciplined by their father?"

Hebrews 12:8 "If you are not disciplined – and everyone undergoes discipline – then you are illegitimate, not true sons and daughters at all."

Romans 12:12 "Be joyful in hope, patient in affliction, and faithful in prayer."

Matthew 5:11 "Blessed are you when people insult you, persecute you, and falsely say all kinds of evil against you because of Me."

Psalm 37:24 "Though he may stumble, he will not fall, for the Lord upholds him with His hand."

THANKFULNESS

Psalm 135:3 "Praise the Lord, for the Lord is good; sing praise to His name, for that is pleasant."

BLESSING

Deuteronomy 1:11 "May the Lord, the God of your ancestors, increase you a thousand times and bless you as He has promised."

APPENDIX

REST AND RENEWAL

Luke 5:16 "But Jesus often withdrew to lonely places and prayed."

Luke 6:12 "One of those days, Jesus went out to a mountainside to pray, and spent the night praying to God."

Mark 6:31 "Then, because so many people were coming and going that they did not even have a chance to eat, He said to them, 'Come with Me by yourselves to a quiet place and get some rest.'"

Matthew 14:23 "After He had dismissed them, He went up on a mountainside by Himself to pray. Later that night, He was there alone."

BIBLIOGRAPHY

Note: In researching the proper use of capitalized pronouns in reference to our Lord, we were surprised to find that this practice seems to have fallen out of favor simply because some modern Biblical translations did not use it. Various authors do not capitalize "he" and "him" when referring to God, Jesus, or the Holy Spirit to maintain consistency in literary style when quoting from these Biblical texts.

We, however, have chosen to use the capital "He" and "Him." How important is "consistency in literary style" when compared to the sacrifice Christ made on the Cross? Surely our Creator, Redeemer, and Sustainer deserves proper pronouns and much more!

References

Andesite Press, August 11, 2015. *Paul's Prose and Other Sermons*, (one of the books Biblical scholars document as the basis of civilization and culture.)

Chambers, Oswald. *My Utmost for His Highest*.
Grand Rapids, MI: Oswald Chambers Publications Association, Ltd., 1992.

Chambers, Oswald. *Oswald Chambers: Abandoned to God*.
Grand Rapid, MI: Oswald Chambers Publications Association, Ltd., 1993.

Cobb, Nancy, and Grigsby, Connie. *The Politically Incorrect Wife*.
Colorado Springs, CO: Multnomah Books, 2000, 2002.

Lewis, C.S. "The Weight of Glory" in *The Weight of Glory and Other Addresses*. New York: HarperOne, 2001; 36, 46.

MacLaren, Alexander. *Paul's Prayers and Other Sermons*, Chapter 1, Page 12.

NASB, *Life Application Study Bible*, Hardcover – Zondervan.

BIBLIOGRAPHY

New American Standard Bible & Life Application Study Bible.

New American Standard Bible® (NASB), Copyright ©
1960,1962, 1963, 1968, 1971, 1972, 1973,1975, 1977, 1995 by
The Lockman Foundation.
Used by permission www.Lockman.org

NIV Life Application Study Bible, Copyright 2011 by Zondervan. All Rights Reserved.

Strauss, Richard L. *Famous Couples of the Bible.*
ISBN 978-0842308366. Carol Stream, Illinois Tyndale House Publishers, January 1, 1993.

The Holy Bible, New International Version ®, NIV ®,
Copyright 1973, 1978, 1984, 2011 by Biblica, Inc. ™ Used by permission. All Rights Reserved Worldwide.

www.ingramcontent.com/pod-product-compliance
Lightning Source LLC
Chambersburg PA
CBHW050439010526
44118CB00013B/1604